KIRIGAMI

KIRIGAMI

Utpal Chakraborty

HAWAKAL

CALCUTTA | NEW DELHI

hawakal
CALCUTTA | NEW DELHI

Hawakal Publishers

33/1/2 K B Sarani, Mall Road, Calcutta 80
70-B/9 Amritpuri, East of Kailash, New Delhi 65

Email info@hawakal.com
Website www.hawakal.com

First edition September, 2020

Cover art: Pinterest
Cover design: Bitan Chakraborty

ISBN: 978-81-934230-2-8

Price: 350 INR | USD 10.99

for
Professor Satiprasad Maiti
&
Kiriti Sengupta

My Pilgrimage

For quite a decade, I have been writing essays and poems on a serious note. But not until a few years ago I thought of shaping them into a book, though my books of academic interest got published in bulk by a publisher based in Calcutta. After having published more than ten books for the students of English language and literature, I was not complacent. Something inside me egged me on to write poems, nonfiction, and fiction. I was confident with nonfiction and essays, but when it came to writing poetry, I stumbled. I felt I was suffering from a lack of nutritious feed on how to compose a fine piece of poetry. Eventually, I understood that writing criticism of a poem is more manageable than composing one. It took me longer to grasp the techniques of writing. But whenever I planned to set a manuscript, I faced bizarre snags. I, however, finally completed one, and as I finished tailoring them to suit a publication, a severe pandemic hit the world. Being shut up in my flat, I thought many of my poems that were related to various seamy aspects of our society, the environmental collapse, the fast erosion of values, and good rituals would lose their relevance. I revised them time and again, penning some of my new insights that this experience of quarantine helped me to thrive on. The *new normal* taught me so many fresh ideas that would otherwise have not been written.

I had a brief meeting with Kiriti Sengupta, and it was he who encouraged me to go ahead. By the time I started making specific edits of some of my poems, written long ago, some pathetic human behavior and the resumed environmental pollution reminded me of those bad bygone days. I could not leave aside the verses I wanted to exclude. After attending the workshop conducted jointly by the Oxford Bookstores and Hawakal Publishers, I focused more on the economy of words.

Finally, the poems get home in the present title, *Kirigami*—a title chosen by the critically acclaimed poet Kiriti Sengupta. My verses are inspired by my very personal experience of the contemporary events—what I see around—my takeaways from an eclectic range of reading on philosophy, science, religion, and human psychology, along with my philosophy of looking into the mysteries of the world. While many celebrated poets have found their muses in different objects and beliefs, I have found mine in my inner self. I write, burning my hands. To me, poetry is a journey from the mundane to the spiritual. Poetry burns oneself and reduces one to his or her purest self, removing all that a poet inherits, giving the artist an evident, unprejudiced eye that can take everything easily and express them readily. A genuine poet like a veteran musician does not make things difficult. They don't indulge in complicated rhythms and tans but express their feelings in a graceful yet lucid manner.

Among other inspirers, I'm indebted to my mentor, respected Satiprasad Maiti, an erudite scholar and a top-rated professor in the department of English of Narendrapur Ramakrishna Mission Residential College. My gratefulness to the Indian scriptures, and WB Yeats, Matthew Arnold, Rabindranath Tagore, T.S. Eliot, Joy Goswami and Shankha Ghosh can never be exaggerated. I hope *Kirigami* will be read across the world.

Utpal Chakraborty
7th of September 2020
Dum Dum, Calcutta

CONTENTS

Nudity	13
Paradise	14
New Normal	15
Metamorphosis	16
Rotation	17
Golden Husks	18
Favourite Teacher	19
Tora	20
Picture	21
Kite	22
A Relief	23
Eternal Tree	24
Patriotism	25
Poverty	26
Dark Hours	27
Squall	28
Cherishing Death	29
A Vision	30
Kirigami	31
It's Not Moon	33
Burglary	34
Emancipation	35
An Eclipse	36
Knee-deep Grass	37
Beloved	38
Striking	39
Void	40
Habitation	41
Seven Floor-Tower	42
Cactus	43
Beacon	44
Dimple	45
Give me Light	46
Divinity	47
Gandhar	48
Seeds	49

Stratosphere 50
Stirs 51
Stroke 52
Grasshopper 53
Train 54
House 55
Nothing 56
Yet I'm Not Ready to Pull Out 57
Suicide 58
Dip 59
Spotlight 60
An Irony 61
Serendipity 62
Surrogate Mother 63
Striped Pyjamas 64
Unethical 65
The Flautist 66
Equal Music 67
A Hornet 68
Soulmate 69
The Sun 70
Complete Works 71
The Advertiser 72
Nothing Ghostly 73
A Platform 74
A White Bird 75
Transition 76
Epiphany 77
Lockdown 78
A Death Trap 79
Addiction 80
Boundary 81
Visually Challenged 82
Negligence 83
Art of Living 84
Speed 85
Flock 86
Sadism 87

Nudity

It will be a longer wait perhaps
till I could take out all the tapestry,
all the ornaments
from the storeroom,
undress a poem
to savour the infantile perfume of the travail.

Paradise

Our childhood paradise sat
on the earthen floor
of our common kitchen.
It circulated through hand fans,
and goose bumps of bedtime stories.
It was smeared in afternoon sports;
one football team easily formed
of the extended family.
It came as a long-waited one set of new dress
on the first day of the pujas.
Bijoya greetings with sweetmeats joined the ends.
On every day before *Dashami*
I still settle disputes, floating lamps
from the seventh floor.

New Normal

Some delicate pores of a Britannia
biscuit steal me.
Through its eyes
I slip into a different galaxy,
see a new sky, a new sun,
shadowless me inside.
All ears to the beatings
of the sinking stars,
a new normal unfolds.
I realise confinement binds.

Metamorphosis

A fair face has been
the yardstick of beauty—
a trillion-year-old prejudice.
It's a periphrasis for
discriminating between flowers.
The real architects
have only dried tears,
which take a long time
to freeze on pitcher plants.

Rotation

Nataraj, the universal maestro
points to us a plethora
of *Soms* continually
But the bulk of them
glides down like
flowing streams
some Picassos catch
a few of the notes
misty shapes of the
fresh roses unreeled
in touches of brush
on the uneven plane
of history bows of earthen Esraj
stand stranded in continuous *tan*.

Golden Husks

Ripening rice sheaves waft.
Everything looks quiet.
They meander through the alleys
fumbling for a few rays in the dark.
Vested mines glow with lewd eyes.
On the day of harvest, a full moon hangs
atop the towering trees,
and in the twilight,
the sheaves are upped and thrashed.
The golden husks have a tryst
with a quack or fall from the hills.
Everything will remain
quiet until the next twilight.
The creek gurgles inside the hills.
And we stand over there,
a bloated packet of humane thoughts.

Favourite Teacher

As I fall to recollect, the name
of my most favourite teacher,
a vibrant village I grew up
with forays into my choice.
He who taught me to avoid a foul,
have a penalty shot and hit the goal.
She who took me to a snake-charmer,
a faith healer and fire.
He who awakened me to the mystery
of the god of football's handball,
undetected by thousands of camera.

Tora

The unbodied thimble of tears
grows, scaling several steps.
As the family deity melts
in the strains, an ikebana on the dais
blooms out of a cluster of notes
on the Rubab's strings;
like a poet, who is born
long after his death.

Picture

Out of your abundance
I lay by one or two colours
as a housewife chooses a jewel.
The one or two of them I store
rarely seems feasible, intelligible.
Still I keep in mind the dewy leaves
after the rain ceases,
store the colourful tehai
of the birds on
the top of the twigs.
touch the throbbing hands
of Picasso and Binoy,
embrace the undefined and the
unknown source of opposite *Jahala*
in the darkening forest.

Kite

I had a craze for flying kites that would soar, singing for days. I proposed to the hard paper I had. She said, "Your song is not exhausted yet." I, an inquisitive Oedipus, decorated you with tinsel insisting on my point. You flashed a smile. When I finally sent it soaring, I felt an intense pull for quite some time. Once the centrifugal force proved higher, leaving me a wet piece of snapped rope in my hand. After a few days, I unlocked my chest to see a colourful flying field in place of *Bimala*.

Note: *Bimala* is a character in the novel called, *Ghare Baire*, written by Rabindranath Tagore.

A Relief

As mask is a precondition now,
I prefer to go out with hair uncombed,
my cheap shirt unsmoothed.
It saves a little time, allowing me
to become myself. I feel easy to walk about,
without the fear of being wrinkled further.
Blessed am I to be unquarantined in a brand factory.

Eternal Tree

As the leaves fall
dementia accumulates like sapsuckers
in the hollows of the tree.

Clouds and rainbows gradually dissipate
from the horns of the deer.

Patriotism

The anonymous traveller sucks
the starch from the footpath to
douse the flame of the pyre.
A fairy carries her immortal dad
on a bicycle, paddling 1500 km on road.
Some angels survive the sorcerer's torture
of exorcising the virus with a disinfectant.
While these carry the national flag into the air,
choppers meet the boozy tables.

Poverty

Absorption into a world
dissolves all differences.
Who can be so rich
to afford the loss?
Poverty is a rich mineral.
Most people are in pursuit of.

Dark Hours

In hours of darkness,
Adrienne said, "Don't be disheartened, man.
Wind blowing through Hemlock trees
can sanitize your mind."
As I stood flummoxed, *Debdas Achariya* shook
me up to say, "When you are on the cross-roads,
brother, don't give up the fight and grab the
ring of diamond that an eclipsed sun leaves behind."

I was about to offer them the flowers of love.
But they all said in chorus, "A human shouldn't be
rewarded for showing humanity. Besides, in an
unhealthy air, petals too seem to hurt a human soul."
I was happy to be offered some rarest jewels
on my journey from one darkness to another.

Squall

When there is a squall in the sky,
don't close the casement.
Let it come and sit on the
cushion of your room.
Let some dust stick to you.
Hug the straws of the broken
nests, water them.
Soon you will find your garden bloom in
counter-stories, and counter-worlds.

Cherishing Death

Wield the darkness.
Set the bird as your Artemis
to chase the pride of jackals.
Let them be hunted one by one.
Meanwhile, you enjoy the game.
Cherish the death of your
dogmatic old software.

A Vision

A fog at long intervals comes
out of the cave perching on
the paws of a black cat.
Through long nights
it strides the six-lane avenue,
eyeing the jutted dentures of the dinosaurs.
I grasp we are trebly quarantined.

Kirigami

1
Could you add affection to glue?
Shake the pillars?
Dissolve the melanin blues?

Hebrew or Greek,
silence or gestures,
don't matter.

Even dews or stories,
poetry or pencil-sketch,
charcoal or *Sarod* doesn't
matter as instrument.

What precipitates is the fabric.
The ziggurat of the broken pieces
of your white paper.

2
Chameleons refuse gravity.
A fly is capable of a 360 degree angle.
While humans invent a duster,
a flower convalesces through the debris.
These are proofs of a single mind.

It's Not Moon

A fresh breath is like a choked log.
A filling meal, homelessness incarnate.
Each poem is a tear for a lost bud;
crest reflecting sharp fall.
A little bit of elixir, poison.
And I avow that I'm not up to a
soft landing on the moon.

Burglary

Right from the start you are known to me. But never grew a proximity between us. Your tricky knocking is intelligible from your furtive droppings of some dark seeds on my door step. I prefer silence and like Frida Kahlo carve out some architectonics of the woods of thorn. One day you turn Lucifer from a mendicant. In a bid to burgle, you squeeze out all the semblance of my being.

Emancipation

After having whizzed far let's now pull up.
Let's disembark to see how the wounded twigs
bank upon their will to shoot up.
Let's look how the earth dolls up on her own
to heal the holes of our bruised sky.
Let's revel in the sky's tears raining
hued lines on the boundless canvas.
Let's observe the emancipation of the
yellowed tales from the underlined
chronicles of our march.

An Eclipse

The Earth quakes.
Rivers break their banks.
Fire burns at random.
The sky gets electrified.
The gentle gale whines into hurricane.
You too lose your equanimity at times.
The trigger is all the same.
An eclipse.

Knee-deep Grass

On my chest is knee-deep grass.
Still I am awake.
Lying down always I
see the sky,
the oceans in euphoria fly.
Upon my head live all corpses
my speech and gesture disallowed
the fest is in my name though.

Beloved

You can cut out a pound of flesh
from my body without spilling
a single drop of blood...
You can pierce my heart
with your sword of tears
and go scot-free...
I'm now blind.
So you can blind me further...
Still I cannot bear with
a Lily on your face.
Do whatever you can
and call me a sinner.
I am the rescuer of your soul, the Ganges...

Striking

We learn to set aside the crutches,
healing from the disease of habits.
We hear the crushing sounds of all
our congenital egos, the whisper of the
verdant, styling the buzz. We learn
a guerrilla war to survive.
We learn our triviality and
taste the worth of sailing together.
But neither Aesop, nor even a scientist
could teach us all these.
We are taught by a short internment,
not by a long one.

Void

Birds flutter in the void: it's but a hearsay.
Void is nowhere.
Since Aryabhatta realized it long ago,
we can now zero in on zero.
Don't think the person you have quarantined
wants emancipation for sleep.
Extend him a colour pencil.
Just peep into his emptiness to
discover a whole new world on the throes of pain.

Habitation

A little room have I.
No window, no door, a fatless sky within.
Neither the wind of spring nor of burns
floats in. Apolitical I, thus stay safe.
Since an equal music, an inner current truss
us, we stay glued unfettered
and with us stay these cave paintings and our
six storeyed edifice.

Seven Floor-Tower

As light sharpens its claws,
all directions are in a shambles.
Seven rings on my five fingers
attract a white horse.
It gallops through the misty arteries,
breaking all the blocks one by one.
The higher it scales, the further
away I walk from the chariot.
A piece of sand and a world of people converge.

Cactus

Everywhere there's the
wind of the rain
of stones. Trees are burnt
out of the arrested heat.
Amidst withered air
Shalgram rocks on the relics.
On them are the skeletons
of some pale potentates.
Yet through meritritous silence,
some hell-bent cactus dig the soil.

Beacon

Despite the lighthouse, some sinking
ships still break the compass.
Dust from sandstorm smears the sky.
Shaking off the boiling syndrome
we get ejected from one ism to the other.
Walls betray the sin of preparing the wicks.

Dimple

Considering that a dimple
they thought about a fest through the day.
Showing the rotten carcass of a rodent
out of fun they made you skip dinner.
Though the dimple deepened,
they didn't recognize your birth sign.
If you try to put a bandage around,
it will loom as a longer line of laughter.

Give me Light

Your *Sarod* is being torn
by the imposed *Pakhoaj*.
On your cushioned stage
is hammering the denture,
methane letting the rope loose.
You are drawing worlds yet.

Divinity

You are the chief priest,
an heiress of your
little temple.
Since your mother's mortal remains
are just consigned to the flame,
you are denied the worship of that benign.
You are now a stained woman,
yet the scripture says, "He is omnipresent."

Gandhar

For long and in multifarious ways
I've looked for *Gandhar*.
Diving into the labyrinth easily,
I've journeyed from burning lava
to sweet home, from Tsunami to shopping mall.
All on a sudden today morning,
I felt uneasy at the clank of utensils in the kitchen.

Note: *Gandhar* or *ga* is a normal note in an octave of
Indian classical music.

Seeds

I was enjoying Amaltas, Hasnuhana,
from single horned Rhinoceros to Periyar.
One pin from the corner of the table
suddenly burst into laughter.
I've trodden that path many times.
But after so many days it came out vocal.
And from my estivation seeds of grain started pouring in.

Stratosphere

The hungry are busy feasting on flesh.
Like Hyenas they suck the yummy ribs.
When their hunger reduces, thirst prolongs.
They search for further drink. Even the ponds
and rivers fail to quench their thirst.
As soon as the sea approaches, they
become Thor in one breath.
Stratosphere, however, keeps
panning its indifferent camera on.

Stirs

Cutting the legs and hands of
some words only continuous
tihai is going on. All 'complete works'
are disappearing like sociolects.
Only some paperback abridged classics
are sitting on the lecture platform.
Everywhere there is great demand
for special effect. I too sometimes
make stirs inside the eggs of winged ants.

Stroke

The chair, the table I sit on to write, the bed I think of lying down suddenly start shaking. Quivers the deed of the plot, the quake proof skyscraper of a very strong base. I start running. By and by the edifice and lamp post fall down to disappear. The surface of the roads rise up as manholes. All flights crush one by one. The fields start breaking. I run, I run along the coastal lines. By that time all the jungles get cleaned. The sea usurps the earth. I keep on running. Everything starts burning. The black holes and the white dwarfs in the process of eating up the stars become small themselves. Soon the myth of the earth reduces into an atom. I myself disappear and await a stroke on the forehead.

Grasshopper

I didn't understand first that the thing I tried to catch so long through the desert, the hills, the seas, the rivers and the jungles was none but a grasshopper standing right in front of my nose. The moment I quivered, it flitted out of my specs to the dance of the rain. Right now it stands still on the stones of my eyes. A strong net in hand I am readying myself for its next leap.

Train

This burnt-out craggy earth is not suitable for the train to pull in. Still the platforms are overcrowded. So many Rilkes and Mayakovskys grapple amidst the nudges and the acid rains. Numberless lamps of science are flanked by shrouds. If on any day I can board it safe, I thank myself. Out of the furnace I enter quickly into the lines of perception.

House

After many arduous assays for long we had got a house. Long after I had had my own room. As an extra window grew up, I saw a quiet tree put its head piercing through the hard floor. I noticed a bird nest in, collecting assorted fruits, eating and wasting.

The other bird sits watching all these in an attitude of indifference. I myself can observe all these. When I ask who I am, who these birds are and what kind of a tree it is, I see some bubbles of light wafting in the air. The particles and the house gradually become Harappa in front of my eyes.

Nothing

In the jungle when the single horned
rhinoceros is a mystery, when the
speedbreakers dash the waves into pieces,
anesthetizing us midway, someone
comes forward to dissolve that labyrinth.
A hitherto frightened audience,
we start clapping in joy.
As the curtain goes up,
the dais becomes conspicuous.
Almost in the last scene in Lear's house
the light of 'nothing' is resplendent.

Yet I'm Not Ready to Pull Out

When I lost my morning, I craved to get it back. When I lost my noon, I felt sad and yearned to fly back and then, I resigned to all sweet reminiscences. When I lost my afternoon, the wizened time came. The sterility that ambushed so long set me on a keel. I willed to move forward. But it did injustice to me. It made me feel I was not prepared. As I lost my hearing, one emissary came to signal, "You are not yet ready to leave the scene." I have been living for years crippled, cabined and bound to a stag. Yet I'm not ready to pull out.

Suicide

When you get nothing of the vinyl,
the festoons of punctuations,
the algorithm of pops,
you feel down and dump
all your harvest as rotten hay.
When someone steals the golden husk
to preserve ice, the world sings a dirge
complimenting your silence as suicide.

Dip

Each moment I duck under the streams of thousands of rivers. After each willed bath floats a corpse. Logically there is left no claimant of that. Caring a straw for it I too look forward to a new dawn. At times one or two whispers, pull one or two of them. I feel hilarious to find me alive among some sounds of arrested silence.

Spotlight

In the spotlight, people see me ensconced in a distant throne. It brings out the razzmatazz of my success, the glare of my being. Chapped toes of the world, mangy skin of the potentials pop up. Float before me across the heap of garlands some sounds that shine their nails with fluorescent colours. *Vuma* makes me eloquent. By and by the light intensifies, revealing every pore of my being, my saliva wrapped in a catapult.

An Irony

I offered a little pariah a meaty,
if, a tad smelly, stale bone.
It ate that he felt owed to me
heavily for the charity.
Trying to lift his forelegs
in a gesture of thanks.
I stood up but my head bent down.
I felt the irony.
Someone confided in my
belittled soul, "Don't worry. You are
not in hell; it's a little purgatory."

Serendipity

Sitting under the big blue sea here on the green carpet I see little starry fishes swimming with a good enterprise to keep me awake. Manna's falling here, the floral veil arresting the freckled flies. I'm very much here. As a new light blinks through the timed chinks, your cheeks glisten with reluctant pangs of abdication. The heavy heart pounds faster to turn nowhere whence a sweet numbness emanates. Your journey is renewed. You exist and you will. Let me sleep as I wish and wish not. Let me cease as I've ceased and yet not. Let me take leave as I've lived longer.

Surrogate Mother

The officer-in-charge
orders the constable
to bring a platter of
mutton biryani with a strong.
The constable demurs.
The officer understands,
gesturing him to do as directed.
The page in the restaurant
gives the parcel, leaning.
The constable waves him.
As the page does not inch out,
the shop owner signs him to resume.
The shopkeepers do their business
on one fourth on the government roads.
And their rapport with the vigilance
is as old as the rocks.

Striped Pyjamas

My neighbour who is also my close friend says that he has given his paternal big pond on lease. The businessmen give the fishes all those food that are nothing but filth. Anyone passing by gets choked by a foul odour. The businessmen catch them and spray all poison that make them look fresh. Even the ice that is used to preserve them is used in the Mortuary. Isn't time ripe for all to put off the striped pyjamas?

Unethical

You have reached the flood- hit people.
You pan on the tremor,
working with the rescuers in tandem.
The executives murmur,
"He is not a journalist, albeit a philanthropist."
"And you have risked your job," says the boss.

The Flautist

Close your eyes and ears,
you would see the mellifluous.
You could see the exploding stars,
frequencies of the prowled innocence,
burgeoning grasses, and their deflowering.
Can you see they lead but to the same tangent,
the bricolage of the master piper?

Equal Music

On one lonely noon under the open sky
we play hide and seek and dive deep into
the waves. One unknown grasshopper pulls
both of us out of the water. After some days
I find one of my selves and you too get one of yours.
Still after a long time the finest of mine finds its match
in one of you. On and around the meeting point
is built up then innumerable cities and oasis.
"Thanks Daniel, court no 19."

A Hornet

Even as a weak hornet lets its
spent wings down on the corridor,
all the folks at home suddenly fall to
shouting out of fear. The housewife
says, "However small or weak, the wasp is
dangerous. Kill it now." In the liquid blood of
the poet then a jumbo jet with a huge
number of crews crush into pieces
with a thunderous sound on the thoroughfare.
While wanting to be still, an impecable sky
grows restless inside the fist.

Soulmate

Stay blessed my only
duchess, the well of love.
You have put off the sheen
of your complexion, eating
with me the spews of mine.
You are absconding along with me
when you know you may embrace
the inexorable earlier than I do.
I see you swaying with me to gift
me what you are laying by...
Whatever you have given me
is white, your emancipation.

I don't know who I'm dear to.
Isn't it better to be friended?

The Sun

Look at the sky, clad
in metaphysical hues.
Look at the text, having
a nose in the air.
Look at the moon,
dressed in calm moments of poetry.
Should they boast of borrowed brilliance?

Complete Works

Even after thirty-two dewy seasons like a ticketless child I slip off from my mother's lap. Managing to sit down with a little bit of ease I slip off each time. Now I cover up winter, now I seek for ice. Just after two or three exercises, I fall from the five-digit-corridor. While having safari on the hills or on the sand dunes I slip off every day. Fresh wind from water comes up to sit with a wrapper on the sympathetic strains. Soon after the sofa becomes empty, fresh chores flock to fill in the gap. My newly published *complete works* seem to be written by some others, a packet of scraps.

The Advertiser

In front of your eyes
I kneel down enthralled,
embracing your leafy banner.
Still in fine I get restless,
keen to scratch the ribs
of your advertisement in
the last go.

Nothing Ghostly

Whether I keep the door ajar or not,
as I dust the floor,
some blurred curls throng around.
Showing up for a very short while,
they stand close to the corners.
Even as I approach them,
they move away like the children,
blushful to see the new guests at home.
The frequency of vanishing the delicate coils
matches the unwinding of the old sore.

A Platform

Trains run with light sparkling on
either side of the railway-track.
The middle remains empty with
some weak spleens. Only a boasting half-
naked woman shouts to break the world
with a single stroke of her finger.
The unequal fight with the night
glues the pauper to the concrete.
Slumber in the evening here continues
unmarred and night walks in for a
routine check up every night.

A White Bird

One painted stork
weathers upheavals
to cross over oceans, and seas.
She is keen to be tanned on an Indian beach without
knowing the health benefits of low melanin.
To be fair to the bone, she falls to peel off her
feathers, beak and claws, groaning in pain.
After a few months she is born to be wooed
by the Drongos again.

Transition

Every moment we resurrect.
Every morning starts an era.
Every day is four eras in brief.
Every life is four eras together.
We are, however, now on a
sponsored tour from untruth to truth.
Let's have a fresh dip with a new insight.
Choice is, after all, not a predestination.

Epiphany

A child enquires, "Which is left and which is right?" The scientist stumbles on crossroads. The seeker giggles. The Earth see-saws in non-finite dimensions. The philosopher gives him an anti-vertigo pill, chanting *Om Namah Shivaya*. I came back to the tramline again.

Lockdown

Windowed skies peep in.
The stars, the hills start
climbing the wall.
Overlooking them
alluring shrouds
cradle some hamlets.
Summer, the sooth-sayer
whispers, "All our trains and avenues,
sourced from these bucolic days detour
into everyone's Malgudi towns."

A Death Trap

A conflict climaxes into catastrophe.
The litterateur burns in friction between
the container and the contained.
Out of the blaze of the *raga Pradip*
we savour *Darbari Kanada*.

Addiction

That man is an addict since the start is an open secret. He is led to Lethe with eternal sedatives. But those morphemes did not do him any harm. Rather they have saved the visionary. The addiction that turned him active is now leaving him inert, indifferent. The fact that he is now busy on android or in the trap of some artificial game is not his own doing. Something else lurks within. All addictions of the world seem to converge and all are stuck somewhere as a housewife is stuck in sari. As the rituals of addiction are restored to sense, I too find myself addicted to fulfil the myriad goals of this apparent offence.

Boundary

Margin is in your hand. You can take it anywhere after your sweet will. The measuring rope is also made after your opinion. So think– would you break the wounded LOC? All enmity broadcast? As the bamboo shoots efface out all the boundaries so if you can go past the measure, you can also be the star. Your diffusion would reach the dark unconditioned and lit up the border. Restriction sounds in the very tune of losing it. That silent journey is quite pure and free from desire, like the unseen tulip smeared in sandal savour. Unnecessary time thus wakes up on the fruitless lines. Only the stars are the connoisseurs of breaking the bounds.

Visually Challenged

Hotels turn homestay overnight, nursing homes, hospitals in writing. Opinions too follow; duties freeze in the hands of the administrator. While roads get full of bumps, strikes gauge the depth of water. Files lie scattered behind the heaps of paper. The hunted know the trick. They move about shops. When the tug of war ends, voracious mountains spread their wings. When public opinion awaits voluntary death, people dance to the beatings of deafening drums. Addicted mass recourses the taught blind alleys. After the pujas the structure is nothing but trash. Commodification shuts eyes to walk in royal fashion, while the blind in the dark ruins the blind's passion.

Negligence

Weakening me in the latent heat of connivance, you wanted to smear me on your lips mixing with sauce. You did spare no pains to do it. But you didn't think that the withered faggot in the heat might yield beautiful result. In fact you didn't surmise that the antonym of heat is also the suppression of heat. See in my little journey an illustrated proof. In the lines of my hand is obvious the magic wand. The longer the distance, the deeper the scattering of the grace across the horizon. Little are its lapses and errors. Calm winter is belched out by beloved negligence. Intense rays of the full moon open up my lost sense.

Art of Living

Like the blown tin frame of a Maruti car, you,
the feeble false tiger brandish
your colourful moustache,
and fragile muscle.
It is behind the paper that you
have dug your own cave.
A true forester has a wooden saw in his hand.
Scared of wild beasts and darkness you keep vigil
on death and disease. Your helplessness is your
suicidal sword. Your stamina, fuelled by your passion,
breaks into pieces by attacks and counter-attacks.
Wild beasts unitedly push you out of the cave
into the forest. Those whom you call wild animals
or hated beasts of prey will now teach you
the courtesy, the art of living and staying gay.

Speed

Long-distance trains always
lose weight through acceleration.
Riding one I too realise
the meaning of speed.
Both the hare and the tortoise tread
the same path without the duet.
The tree also takes its time to beget flowers.
Everything runs at its own unit.
To take the mind off the body,
I too run from one work to the other.
The more I get lightened,
the more I find myself out.
This is how I lengthen my life
and stay awake in the body of the mind.
The speed I'm in for ages,
I know the world in brief is getting crowded
with the fruits of that grief.

Flock

While going in a flock every day
I come out of it, returning to my own stillness.
From a distance I see the leader
of the birds descend.
Descends fresh reaction—
some cold isms disappear.

Development mirrors the submerged
concocted boulder. The river breaks its bank
to the dictates of the leader.
The staircase that is bedecked with colourful tubs
carry alien trees. Leaving the country and the time,
opportunity decorates the dais.

Sadism

All day long the sound of tram and its lines strike me coarse. It feels all knives have lost their edge. My reflex seems shrivelled in all where I lose my leg. As if I rotate round the same planet like an inert object. After a thousand decades suns rise and clouds are formed. And there comes rain in all points. Rapture runs riot on the sun of temperance to hide your barrenness. Melt all those snags. I'm only trampled mid-way under the crowd of the rapists. Blood falls down the cheeks of time like waterfalls. A group of schizophrenics make *tans* on the *mir* of pain. Some ventriloquists come to protect the honour. Nice paths get blocked by the incessant tuneless sounds. Mouths of the ruled stand gagged with the fallout of sadism.

www.ingramcontent.com/pod-product-compliance
Lightning Source LLC
LaVergne TN
LVHW091617170726
843492LV00007B/2460